You Could Fly an Airplane

Planning to be a Pilot for Kids

How Airplanes Work

Children's Aeronautics & Astronautics Books

BABY PROFESSOR

EDUCATION KIDS

HOW DO PLANES FLY?

Have you tried
traveling to a
faraway place?

A place where you have to ride a plane to reach your destination?

Have you ever thought
about of how a plane flies?

Here are the things you should know about flying Planes.

Wilbur
The Wright Brothe

We should be
thankful to the
Wright brothers for
inventing the plane.

A plane has a
strong engine that
helps it fly. The
powerful engine is
pushes the plane
forward, allowing
its wings to create
a lift to stay in
the sky.

Aside from its
powerful engine,
a plane flies
with the help of
air, too.

The air flow is
fast above the
wings which
makes the air go
down towards
the ground
and keeps the
planes in the air.

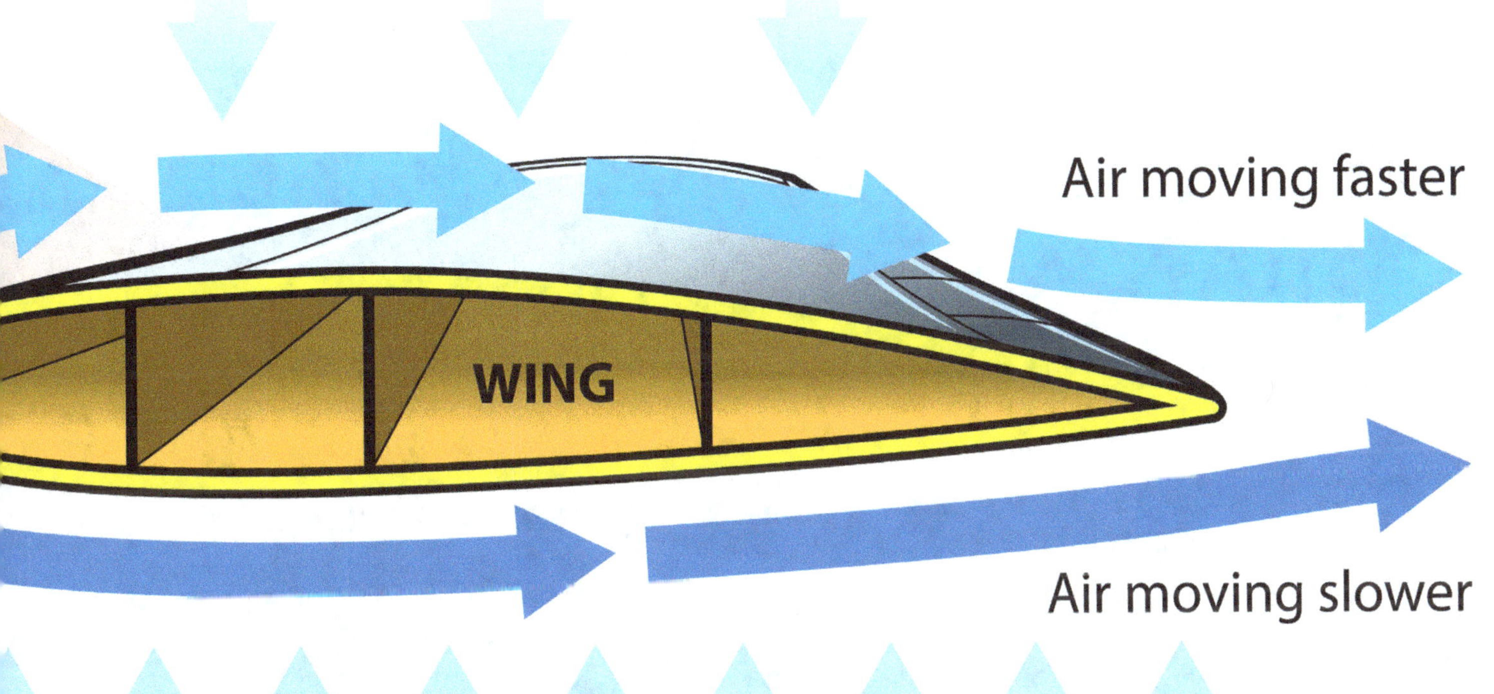

Low pressure
Air moving faster
WING
Air moving slower
High pressure

On the back
of each wing
is an **aileron**,
which helps the
airplane turn
right or left.

The body of an
airplane is called
the fuselage.

The airplanes have a data recorder. Although the data recorded is bright orange in color, it still called "the black box."

The wings lift
the plane and
keep it in the sky.

How do planes know which way to go?

People called
pilots drive the
airplanes.

Pilots have to contact the airport by using a radiophone to know where it's safe to take off and land.

The airport
has long roads
which are called
runways for
the airplanes to
take-off.

Airplanes need
to travel very
far along the
runway before
they can take-
off up into
the air.

When an airplane
takes off you
need to wear
your seatbelt.

Now you know
how planes fly!

Don't Forget to share this book to your friends!

Visit

BABY PROFESSOR
EDUCATION KIDS

www.BabyProfessorBooks.com
to download Free Baby Professor eBooks
and view our catalog of new and exciting
Children's Books

www.ingramcontent.com/pod-product-compliance
Lightning Source LLC
Chambersburg PA
CBHW060146120726
48003CB00009B/3039